T0194028

Journey of Epilepsy

JESSICA MARKIEWICZ

authorHOUSE®

AuthorHouse™
1663 Liberty Drive
Bloomington, IN 47403
www.authorhouse.com
Phone: 1 (800) 839-8640

Published by AuthorHouse 07/07/2020

ISBN: 978-1-7283-6589-3 (sc)
ISBN: 978-1-7283-6588-6 (e)

Print information available on the last page.

This book is printed on acid-free paper.

Seizure Free

Look into the world around you
And what do you begin to see
I see no one had a clue
When I had to beg and plea
Fighting for the helps and needs
As people began to nod
When I overcame the odds

As I began fighting for my life
I felt like I been hit with a knife
The tears and pain it came with
I would eventually know it's not a myth
When I could rest my mind assure
Knowing that this would be a cure
To ending my seizure condition

Knowing today I survived brain surgery
I would take this as my treasury
To begin to learn and grow
And to give out what I could show
For the woman I have become
I will continue to beat the drum
As I live my life seizure free

Seizures

My eyes glowing with tears
That haven't begun to fall
I'm crying from the inside
When you are unable to see
My condition building in fear
Causing me to begin to stall
With nothing but the blind side
For when it's time to begin to flea
From my seizure condition

Many tears shedding in the dark
Being hidden away in my thoughts
With no coverage to speak of my pain
As you would not begin to understand
When all this would leave a mark
Forcing things to come to a halt
For when this would become a drain
And my dreams would become a wonderland
Wishing my seizures to go away

The Unknown

Nobody knows the feel
When living in nothing but fear
As I never know my next seizure
And anxiety haunts my daily life
For trying to live my life free

The time would be so unreal
As my time came so near
And would have some leisure
When I'm living the wildlife
When I no longer have to plea

When She Comes

I'm floating in outer space
The feel of disconnection
As if there no return to earth
For the feel of the ground
Building the feel of fear
As to when this will all end

The few minutes during this time
Seems to last so long
As there is no end to it
When everything comes to a stop
And becomes nothing but a blur
Before coming back to life's reality

The feel of floating on clouds
The sounds and visions begin to go
When there is no stopping this
For its moment to come and go
During these long lasting seconds
As if there is no end for my episodes

Seized

A new center gravity
Forming within the gut
Pulling my weight in from all angles

Electricity firing millions of neurons
As a lightening show begins
Throughout the paths of the brain

My heart begins to race
As anxiety begins to increase
And unable to stop any of this

A new darkness comes upon
As my eyes become useless
Stalling behind the sockets

My ears become blocked
When asked if you need help
Until the lights can be seized

The Struggle

Shaking, twitching, losing control
I don't know when this began
But honestly this is getting really old
As I feel as if no one understands
The struggles seizures come with
When others think it's all a myth

I beg, I beg, please console
As my aura's begun to take control
For the moments begin to drown
And wish for all this to be gone
For I begin to find an end someday
To finding the end of the roadway

The Aura Effect

Aura's begin floating around
For the moment of déjà vu
I begin falling to the ground
Faster than gravitational acceleration
Body jerks like an earthquake
Mind and body go separate ways
As I have no control

Electricity strikes within
With no control of my abilities
To take control of my muscle's strengths
As you dare not to touch me
Only to let me begin to reunite
With my body and mind during this time
For God could only explain these episodes

The Darkness

Deep into that darkness, I stood alone
The feeling left when I felt disowned
I'm left with fear, doubt and dreaming
As the inside of my body is screaming
When these feelings become so strange
For the dream's I'd have a life change
As this wouldn't be something to ignore
No mortal to ever dared to dream before

Invisible

My heart begins racing
My body begins to tremble
As I begin to float upon
The clouds from above
I begin to face the unknown
When the auras begin to set

My mind continues spacing
As I try to resemble
When something to dwell on
For I've become beloved
For that I am not alone
During this darkness time I have met

I begin to find my way
Back from the invisible dark side
To continuing to live my life in drive
For I continue to pray
To God to help me lead and guide
As I live my life invisibly and strive

Aura's

Feeling of numbness within my body
My senses begin to fade away
For the increase of anxiety or fear
As I feel separated from myself
When I feel the lifting from above
Continuing to float above the clouds
As there is no ending to my episode
During the longest lasting minutes
In the moments of being in déjà vu
Before retuning back to the grounds
As my seizure comes to an end
And the hallucinations begin to fade away

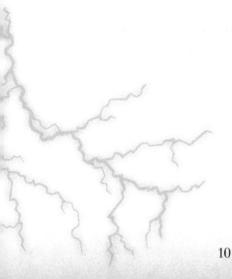

Imagine

Image yourself floating upon clouds
As you enter a déjà vu moment
For the escape from the sense of auras
Coming from nowhere sneaking upon
The moment of having a seizure episode
When fear and anxiety begin to build
Without the known of your next seizure
Stopping you from moving forward
As this would slow you down during
The longest few moments lasting forever
Before finding yourself coming back within
To knowing your surroundings again
When you imagine the feel of having seizures

Nobody Knows Me

Nobody knows the real me
When I wanted to be let free
As I sat in my room and cried
When I had to take my tears and hide
I've lost hope when I was let down
Sitting in the lonely room left to frown
No one understood the pain
That left me to become drained
Nothing could explain the feel of overloads
Through every second of my episodes
Not knowing my future ahead
That one day I'd become seizure free instead
Now I stand here seizure free
As I no longer have to plea
To taking my memories to create a plague
When I no longer have to look back
As I begin to live my life seizure free

Pretending

Pretending to be happy when you're in pain
Time for you take, learn, and gain
Even during times that may seem to worsen
Shows how strong you are as a person
When people know your condition
Only gives you to find your position
When those begin to fear you
When unknown what to do
We seized not the soul
As being seizure free becomes a goal

Epilepsy

E is for Epilepsy Awareness
P is for prayer to the end of our condition
I is for isolation from activities
L is for learning how to cope and teach
E is for electrical firing in the brain
P is for positivity and healthy results
S is for shaking and tremors
Y is for yearning to put an end to this

I had Epilepsy and...

I am an epilepsy warrior
I am a survivor
I love to tell my story
I am seizure free
I am a believer
I run for a purpose
I am a fighter
I am a person
I have faith

Epilepsy Dreams of Freedom

I had epilepsy seizures in my life
However, here I am still alive
Obscure force constantly attacking me
Causing me to fall to my knees
The force pushing me against gravity
When I pray God for serenity

Epilepsy you have been with me
But it is now time to flee
Things are no longer blurry
For I will no longer have to worry
I begin accepting the applauds
As I overcame the odds

Don't Be Afraid

When down get up and dance
As every morning is a new chance
We get up and begin our day
Even when things seem so grey
Move away from that standing tree
And appreciate every moment seizure free
As the seizures feel so violent
Let our hopes be no longer silent
Let your words be spoken
When these moments make you feel broken

I'm Still Alive

I only live once
To let me make my bunce
As for one day I will die
As my spirits are lifted in the sky
For I live my life still alive

I am here today
As you begin to make way
For me to tell my story
I look out and begin to spree
As I begin my life seizure free

Begin living in a wildlife
I would soon begin a new life
For I no longer have no fear
As the end of the road becomes so clear
For I live my life still alive

Hope Springs Eternal Healing

Hope springs eternal healing
For hard times we are feeling
As we begin to find our place
And begin to take and embrace
For the end of my seizure condition
As it ends in a sense of remission
For he has done my repairs
And answered all my prayers
Now my seizures came to an end
I begin to look upon his glory
As I begin to tell my story

Take My Hand

Take my hand and walk
Through the life given to us
For I want you to understand
As this was not planned
When a seizure begins to creep
Up onto your daily plans
When you and others don't know
The torcher that seizures give us
From living a normal life
But take my hand and don't let go
As the seizures will come to an end
Stand beside me and be my friend
For we will fight through this together

What's In My Head

What's in my head
I want to know
Why in a moment
Everything becomes so grey
As I'm no longer one
For I float in a world
Where I don't belong
Before returning back
To where I am from
As I find my place
Once again after this
Episode from living my life
For I continue to find answers
To my prayers and questions
With what's in my head

The Dark Side

I feel it coming within
The same place it has been
It finds me out of place
For nowhere to chase
As my heart begins to sprint
All this becomes nothing but a hint

She begins to get closer
As I been hit with a bulldozer
A familiar feel begins within
As all these feelings has been
For these pushes me to the ground
When there is no longer any sound

There is no stopping it now
For this becomes a quick powwow
I ask for nothing more
When this leaves me on the floor
I pray for you to be on my side
As this strip me from my pride

These episodes begin to wipe me out
As if I wanted to shout
When it strips me away from my soul
For it begins to take a toll
When it only lasts a minute or two
You would never have a clue

Inhale, Exhale

Inhale, exhale
Count to ten
Count again
And once again
Slow your pulse
Slow your mind
Steady hands
Just in time

Experience of a Seizure

Having a 106° fever
When nothing but a baby
Looking around at everything
Unable to make any decisions
When things become so strange
For a change comes with new additions

You will once become a believer
That there will be such a maybe
When beginning to look at the whole thing
As when everything seems like a collision
And time to make life changes
As I start this seizure condition

Lessons Taught

Every morning is a new day
To pray to God for answers
For I continue to be patient
That I would be seizure free
To live my life free from worry
As this gave me acceptance
For who I have become
And grown to be a woman
Who can grow to tell her story
During the struggles as a kid
When others didn't understand
How my condition would change
My life perks and focus
On what truly matters to me
For the day that my prayers
Would once be answered
And I could continue living my life
To becoming seizure free

If You Ask Me

If you ask me what my dreams are
My mind would draw a blank
As I wish to dream with my eyes open
For it gives me room to think
As time begins to take its part
And the memories begin to fly away
For when you begin to ask me
Reasoning behind my tears building up
For I have no control within
As you many never understand me
For what my life dreams have become
As you continue to ask me about my dreams

What Left Behind

If you look at her closely
You can see the marks left behind
As she has become lost in the world
With nowhere to turn but
The greeting of the flat floor
For this world has become silenced
When this moment has approached me
And my mind begins to unwind
As my body begins to become curled
For I get a feeling within my gut
As I wish this no more
And I continue seeking for guidance
That I will soon find myself recovering slowly
As my condition has been so unkind
For the feeling of being hurled
When I begin to close the door shut
After letting my condition out the door
For when you begin to see me smiling again

I Would Rather

I would rather be human than a tree

I would rather live my life free
To move with the breeze of the wind
For the tree branch can move and
Live its life of worry free

Living my life seizure free
Will once feel like living its life
Like a treat in its forest
As I rather live my life free to be

From the worry when I became seizure free

Uncertainty

I walked in the kitchen to get a drink
I wake up on the floor unable to think
My head begins to spin
As my confusion begins setting in
For I become unsure to what just happened
When people would never imagine

Imagining sitting on the floor unable to move
When people around you had no clue
How to give me some type of support
To give me relief and comfort
During these rough times and moments
As my words are unable to be spoken

For I overcome a moment and came out
As I feel that I want to shout
When I have to beg and plea
In order to get the helps and needs
For everything around is hovering
As I find my place and begin recovering

Why Epilepsy?

Why do I cry? Why do I hurt?
I don't know how to feel when covered in dirt
It never would begin to occur to me
When I didn't know where to start
As this would really break my heart

Epilepsy has become so painful
When feeling life has become a wasteful
My heart begins to ache inside and out
And show that I became a strong fighter

I used to think that this was all my fault
When everything would come to a halt
For I had no control over this
As this time would come with a mighty cost
When I feel confused as my memory has been lost

My seizures caused me to black out
When I filled my life full of doubt
As this has become part of my life
Please don't take the things that matter
For I begin to put an end to this chapter

My Brain Has An 'Episode'

A hand to hold that's all I ask
No need to fuss during this task
When being asked for you to stay
As my brain begins to go grey
When my brain has an 'episode'

It became a lonely place to be
Where there's just my brain and me
In the lonely and weird place
For its times I begin to face
When my brain has an 'episode'

Be on my side for I feel this pain
As my tears begin to rain
For my time has come to a delay
And my memory begins to fade away
When my brain has an 'episode'

Don't be alarmed and just take my hand
As this has become unplanned
Its soon to be over once again
For you can no longer complain
When my brain has an 'episode'

I'm a Person

In the shadows of day and night
In my darkness I must continue to fight
For I will not live my life in shame
As this has not become a game
Please don't begin to freak
When my brain is unable to let me speak
Just stay calm and continue to wait
For these times I began to really hate
I ask nothing but for a helping hand
As these moments are never planned
And yes, I had epilepsy. This is true.
But I am still a person, just like you.

Invisible Day

Day after day
I fought a good fight
So, I have earned my rights
When I felt though
As you may not know
When feeling weak and broken
Leaving me smiles unspoken
When in need to cry

As tomorrow begins to come
I pray for a better outcome
As my pain and suffering will be removed
And my life begins to improve
I pray for all this to end
For when I gain a hand from a friend
As my invisible days come to a rest

Storm is Over

Once again, this storm is over
When leaving me with a hangover
Unable to remember how I made it through
If I only wish you only knew
On how I would be here still alive
For when you learn how I survived
As you may be unsure when the storm will end
When this all feels like nothing but a trend
But as this storm leaves a scar
Remember for who you are
And never stop beating on that drum
For the storms you have overcome

The Cruel Moment

It is a good day everything seemed so perfect
The sky is blue, sun is shining
What could possibly go wrong?
Until I felt you coming
Like a road rage driver creeping up on me

Oh, how I wish for this to be a false alarm
Which you have come to seizure me again
Within the spare of my moment
When you came like a thief in the wind
Beginning to hijack my mind without spare

For any awareness to my surroundings
As this beautiful day has come crashing down
Once again during these terrible moments

I Am...

I am braver because I have won
A battle you could never imagine
Dealing with from a very young age
To become who I am today

I am stronger because I had to be
I fought through the years gone by
Unsure to when my day was to come
As my prayers would soon be answered
For the hope of becoming seizure free

I am happier because I've learned what matters
I've become who I am today
For I have learned how to cope
With this terrible disease on a daily basis
As I do not wish for this upon anyone

I stand taller because I am a survivor
I fought a long battle for years
To get to where I am today
And begin to tell my story
As I become seizure free

Acceptance

What is there really different to see?
About anyone including me
We are all unique in our own ways
With nothing left to say
For when we begin to hear no sound
As our shaking begins round and round
Thinking about what you see
Instead accept the person and let them be
Step in and try to help
Or else that person can just melt
And begin to get swept away
As I pray for you to just stay

Seizure Time

A time to have a seizure
Becomes a body teaser
As I fall to the ground
Without any sound
Don't get too close
As this is no joke
For this time is no good
Try to help like you should
Please stop your fun
Before you begin to run
And try to help me
When I begin to fall to my knees

The Pain Begins

Pain is spreading everywhere
My body begins its attacks
As there is no control over this
When my mind becomes unaware
During this untimely manner
And my eyes begin to glare
For I lose all my senses
During this terrible moment
When this all becomes unplanned
As my body begins to shake
In desperate attempts to come back
From having an epilepsy seizure
As we pray for an end
To all this taking a toll on our lives
So, we can live free and learn to breath
As the pain begins to leave
When our seizures come to an end

Depression

The symptoms wake him up again
Reaching for the limit of hope and relief
Believing that there is no end
Dreaming for actions to be performed
For he sits in his sadness
And in an aerie despair

Seizures causing his mind to go insane
For he is left in disbelief
As he wishes nothing but to have a friend
Who has ideas to be formed
In order to put an end to his madness
And his mind begins elsewhere
When in the moment of a seizure

A Chance of a Lifetime

Today I hoped to achieve something great
For something many would think a heroic trait
Giving myself to the hopes and needs
With hopes that doctors'
Treatments would succeed
When I appeared as well as I could be
And here was my underlying problem of epilepsy
I suspected what I was to be told
Pray that my seizures will be once controlled
Even though I had to wait for many years
That I would realize that id no longer have to fear

I sit back and not let myself be stressed
As I know that I have just been blessed
For I knew what needed to be done
I would never wish this upon anyone
As this seemed a setback for some
I still had a chance for a lifetime to come
I wait for my path to open for me
As my new life has yet to be seen
For my seizures has gone away
I can now live my life on the freeway

The Little Girl

Once upon a time going back
There was a little girl with epilepsy
Growing up for many years with uncertainty
That there would ever be an end
From the unexpected triggers
Crawling through my body
From any unexpected moment in time
On a day to day basis
As I would continue my treatments
And continue many more testing
As if there would be no end
To the darkness of this tunnel
Until God will once grant my wish
To finding a solution to my conditions
When a doctor knew the cause and
Will forever put an end to my years
Of suffering and pain that it came with
When dealing with seizures
Throughout my childhood years
And will once learn to live my life seizure free

I Am Me... Set Me Free

My family never knew what to do with me
I was an obligation that needed to be
But I knew that they loved me indeed
My mom would lay on her knees
Praying to God to beg and plea
As many people would disagree
That one day I would become seizure free
And begin to swim out in the open sea
And my seizures will once become carefree

Why Me?

Playing outside on a hot Summer day
Next on the grassy lawn I stay there and lay
Watching other kids sitting there laughing
As I wondered to myself on what just happened
And I ask myself on why this happens now
For I wish I could overcome this somehow

The days came and the nights went
Thinking to myself, how my time has been spent
When others thought I used to fake
When a seizure used to make me shake
And get tingling trickling down my spine
I would get up and tell them I am fine

A lot of people helped me fight through
I had to stay strong and help myself too
Don't ask questions to how or why
Be positive and strong and don't let yourself cry
What doesn't kill you makes you stronger
So, smile, laugh and sing that little bit longer

I Have Epilepsy Seizures

No, I'm not stupid or mentally disabled
Yes, I am aware of my condition
And no, I am not making this up
Just because my seizures aren't always visible
Doesn't mean they do not exist
I am a person just like you
I may need help from time to time
But I can do many things on my own
Please don't take this as my weakness
That I do not have control over this
For a seizure may come upon with no warning
Having seizures have taken a toll on me
For I am a strong fighter and will try my best
To bring upon those smiles through the pain
So be kind and be supportive to understanding
That you may never know or understand
The smallest acts of kindness from you
That could brighten anyone's day

An Aura Feeling

The symptoms are coming
My stomach begins humming
For everything become flatten
Not knowing what will happen
As this gives an unsettling feeling
To what I and dealing
With these feelings being so strange
Unable to describe this change
For a seizure is to come
As this may be unsettling for some

The Unknown Change

It all changes in a flash
Feeling left in a disturbing clash
The life I knew will once be gone
When told to just hang on
As things would never be the same
For my seizure would be to blame
As they came out of the blue
The times I had no clue
When my days would be numbered
As this disease will be conquered

Journey of Epilepsy

Not everyone will understand
The journey you are in
You are a fighter within
It's not their journey
To judge and make sense of
It is up to you live life
To the fullest through ups and downs
Through thick and thin
As this battle will come to an end
For we continue our prayers
And live our lives journey
During out fight with epilepsy

Be On My Side

Yes, I am a strong person
Even when my condition worsens
Not knowing for when or where
But every now and then
I need someone to take my hand
Take me and help me stand
And take me away
To tell me everything will be ok

The Invisible Illness

When you have an invisible illness
Leaving you behind in a stillness
Hard to explain when they had no clue
For they are not stepping in your shoes
As they are unable to click
Just because you don't look sick
It's a daily struggle to be in pain
For they are unaware the strengths to gain
When they begin to judge you outside
They become unaware of what's inside
As they are told not to judge the book by its cover
For a new thing that they will once discover
When I will no longer have to beg or plea
For the day that I become seizure free

An Aura

My heart and mind begin to race
As my body begins to embrace
For my muscles begin to flex
Unsure to what will happen next
When my body becomes tingling and numb
And this becomes unsettling for some
My vision becomes nothing but a blur
As a seizure is about to occur
My senses become out of whack
Leading me without a track
Racing thoughts, déjà vu
Leaving me behind with nothing to do
But to let the symptoms begin to sing
And the seizure does its thing

I Wish...

I wish people would only know
That I don't discuss my health issues
For pity, sympathy or attention
Instead I wish people knew
How much this has become a part of my life
Whether I want it to be or not
I talk about it due to my experience
To inform and educated others
Not to be looked down upon or judged
But instead to bring awareness
To others about dealing with my disease
And how I became seizure free

Do Not Judge

Do not judge a girl on what you see
She may be fighting cancer, or incurable disease
A little girl comes in many different forms
As she may be facing life obstacles
For this all may seem impossible
She is here, but a part of her is missing
When she takes the battle and continues winning
But if you can take a moment
As this becomes your life's token
And becomes a new lifestyle
To look beyond the smile
With a whole new degree
You might see that the girl is me

She Falls Again

Here the floor she lies
On the cold stall floor
No support from all her weight
For her muscles begin to twitch
As she looked up into their eyes
Begging and pleading for their help
To put this to an end and to a rest
When she begins gaining her strength
Once again back on her feet
And continues to live her life
When the sudden moments take us
From the freedom of God's life given

I'm Lost

Cut down and worry again
Lie here the pillars of my stability
And nothing but the concrete floors
And my senses begin to fade
With no sense of my surroundings
As my seizure takes time from me
Blistering through the body
When there becomes no way out

For this has gave me a delay
And caused a total immobility
Don't be afraid to brining me to stores
What you will begin to face
When they wished you'd just stayed
To gather all their belongings
And pray one day becomes that somebody
To live and not have to miss out

The Suffer In My Eyes

I looked at myself in the mirror
Only to see my smile in an error
The tears hide in the corner of my eyes
Wondering if this just me or all a lie

As I try to make myself look nice
Wonder if its someone in a disguise
For I sit down and take up space
When my emotions are not expressed on my face

Day by day I feel racing in my heart
For my condition tears me apart
When I begin to tell my story
And live my life full of glory

Time flew, leaving memories behind
When this condition has been so unkind
As people asked, "How I was?"
I replied "I'm great" without a pause

Left Behind

Leaving me with little places to go
I sit there and lay low
As I wait for my seizure to take its time
Listening to my voice whistle and hiss
When this becomes something, I wouldn't miss
Sitting on the floor over here
For my dark time ends this year
As you begin listening to my word
And my prayers begin to get heard

The Racing Storm

The sky becomes dark and gray
As this aura begins to find its way
For this storm begins to take its place
And my heart begins to race
When nature's storms seem so severe
Which has always been so feared
For what symptoms it has brought
Epilepsy seizure has always been my thoughts
Lightning strikes across the sky
Seeing how quickly it can pass by
Like the storm in my brain
For when I feel all the pain
Unsure of its severity and length
Depending on all its strength
I'd hope for the end to come sooner
As I become unaware of the future
For I wait for her to perform
And the end comes from this storm

Here We Go Again

A moment in spare brings silence
Eerie feelings begin spreading
The sense of loneliness sinks in
Tingling creeping along my body

Tired, I start to tremble
As an aura begins to reappear
I gather my thoughts to overcome
As I become aware and stay calm

These illusions seem so near
As my conscious builds in fear
For alarming thoughts begin to flow
I pray the only way I know

Lord give me strength within me
For more faith in you I begin to seek
Touch me with your healing hands
And take away all my pain

The strength of his prayers
Healing me from the inside from
The strange feeling of uneasiness
For the time I come back to reality

Keep Your Faith

The sky becomes so bright
As this becomes a wonderful sight
When we pray for some hope
During times we learn to cope
As we place ourselves on the spot
Whether your seizures are controlled or not
For something you are dealing
When praying for some type of healing
And the news begins to arrive
As changes come to our new lives
For medications are not a cure
And sometimes the results are unsure
We can all understand
If we all lend each other a lending hand
Standing together straight and tall
Work together to avoid that great big fall

The Daily Life

The regular daily lifestyle
Will soon be changed in seconds
For what has become a bumpy ride
With what a young child has become
During the diagnosis at a very young age
Too young to understand the intensity
As epilepsy causes major changes
In a person's ability towards life
As a baby grows to be this little girl
Too young to understand her condition
For it has become part of her life
Through the ups and downs with emotions
To pre- judging her disability from
Her differences from others around her
She has grown to be a beautiful young lady
And eventually find a cure to her condition
That would soon put an end to epilepsy
For this little girl who is me

The Storm In My Brain

Standing outside in the stormy day
Watching the lightning strikes
Moving across the gloomy sky
Resembling the waves of an EEG
As the energy waves are released
From the brain's electrical activity
As electricity strikes part of my brain
And my body begins seizing up
Beginning to take over its control
With everything you do
Takes control of your vital organs
Unable to stop its episode
As the lightning begins striking
In the lobes of the brain

Seizure Time

An aura symptomatic feeling begins
As my head begins to spin
I'm on the ground sitting still
For this is not my skill
A seizure time I begin to face
When I begin to feel out of place
And my body begins to recognize
As a seizure intensifies
For this doesn't become a new phase
And leaving my mind in its daze
Deciding on the severity of its own ways
For I wish this to come to an end one day
When I can continue on the go
And show you I'm not slow
Even when a seizure may seem so long
I can show you how I became strong
As this may seem nothing but a breeze
When this condition can be cured with such ease

Set Me Free

Gazing upon from a distance
Oh, how I wish against your existence
When this becomes hard to be controlled
As many stories remain untold
The intensity is not always clear
For every seizure result in great fear
Especially when epilepsy sets in
And the aura feelings are within
My condition would not be known
If my symptoms were not shown
When epilepsy becomes my new domain
As it begins its striking time once again
And the electricity strikes through my brain
As it becomes heavy like a "ball and chain"
This ball and chain may slow me down
But will not stop me from being a clown
Days may feel hard to live through
But the ball and chain can be removed from you

The Truth To Be Found

Lying in bed unable move
Doctors surrounds you
Shining lights into your eyes
Unable to understand the moment
Of truth to be found within
For the diagnosis is upon
The results found from their test
As epilepsy begins to sink in
And the triggers begin to spasm
For I pray for that one day
That this would all come to an end
And ending my seizure condition
When I can say I have ended my fight
With a terrible condition
And learn to live a new life
To becoming seizure free

Keep On Praying

Days go by so ever fast
As our time forever last
When the truth is being told
And I give you my hand to hold
For I ask nothing but you to stay
To join with me and begin to pray
Showing me your true love
Learning about our God above
As you look into my seizure eyes
For I feel it time for me to cry
When my condition leaves me with scars
And I begin looking upon the stars
Holding back those watery tears
When I hope for no more fears
For I have to beg and plea
Oh, seizures let me be free

There You Go Again

There you go again
Continuing to harass me
With your old controlling ways
As this puts a delay to my day
When I feel no end to this

There you go again
Controlling what I do
To make me stay with you
As you send triggers through
My body and soul within

There you go again
Making me feel worthless
When unable to move around
For you cause my body to seize
And stop me from my doings

There you go again
For you have controlled my life
Leaving me with nothing but scars
As you wounded me with a knife
Stopping me from living my life

There was a time I handled you
For when you became so intense
For I would come back fighting
Again, and again to the very end
When I no longer will have any seizures

One Day

I don't look sick you say
I didn't choose to live life this way
This illness you cannot see
When this begins to take away from me
This illness is driving me insane
As this leads my life in great sadness and pain
And my brain begins to freak
As my mind becomes foggy and weak
Floating in the sky's mist
When this will never be missed
For the time we will spend
As this condition comes to an end
When my body feels so sore
For I deserve so much more
So, walk in my shoes for a day
I promise I'll trade you any day

The Unknown Sight

You may not see it
But I can feel it
You may not understand it
But it's what I know
And how I learn to cope
With dealing with it
On a daily basis...

Please don't think I'm lazy
Or feel sorry for me
As I am stronger than ever
I continue my fight every day
To get treated with respect
As I continue to live
My life with epilepsy seizures

Today Is A New Day

Yesterday I felt okay
As today becomes a new day
And I am forced to strap in
For I am unsure what will happen
What this will all bring
As I wish this wasn't a thing
And felt I committed a crime
And begin to learn to serve my time
One day I will no longer miss this
To finding my wisdom in my bliss
For you are unable to see
When my seizures are no longer with me
As you have never walked in my shoes
With what I have been through

It Does Exist

Just because you can't see it
Doesn't mean it not there
And doesn't mean it doesn't exist
I am an epilepsy survivor
Who has fought long and hard
For a very long time in my life
As I wish for you to walk in my shoes
To understand what I go through
When the unexpected begins to occur
And my muscles begin to spasm
As if there is no end to this
And my memory becomes all fog
For the few minutes it begins to last
Until I return to normal reality
And continue to live my life until
The next seizure begins to appear
As there may be multiple per day
When left with nothing left to say

Some Days

They tell me life's a journey
As I get pulled on the gurney
Some days are filled with laughter
While some are filled with tears
As this has taken many years

No one has walked in my shoes
When I share my experience with you
As you are unable to live your life free
Before the time you become seizure free
For you may just never understand

Some days I fear this would reappear
When I'm alone and no one is here
For I may need someone to help me
As I wish you could only see
For what these seizures do

Some days I struggle to move on
As some of my memory is now gone
Only for me to have flashbacks
During my time of looking back
For what I have been through
With my struggles with epilepsy

I Am Free

Don't grieve for me
For now, I am free
I'm following the path
As I lay in my own bath
I sit to avoid that great big fall
When I turned my back and left it all

I could not stay another day
As I had to find my own way
For the life I have earned
When it all became too much
And my heart will once be touched

Begin to lift your hearts
As you look over my charts
When you become blown away
And this all becomes a good day
For you begin to let me be
As I become seizure free

Never Forgotten

I think of things you used to say
At some point, every single day
Even if you knew what I went through
You've never walked in my shoes
How seizures would affect me
Symptoms of aura's your unable to see
For one day my days won't be so bad
When you will once be glad
And you can once let yourself relax
As all this goes behind out backs

Thank You

I know you have many besides me
You helped me with an important key
To look forward without a glance
And give me and my life a second chance
Grateful for what I've been through
As many others may not have a clue
For a much stronger woman I have become
Unsure of what would be the outcome
I can now live my life day in and day out
For many people didn't know nothing about
"Thank you" is what I wish to say
Because of you, I became this way today

Awareness

Epilepsy is something to be spoken about
As many will have a lot of doubt
When this leaves so many scars
For nothing has been done yet so far
And people hope to have a good day
So, they can tell people what they want to say
As some people will never know how
To step back and begin to bow
And spread the importance
Of the awareness of epilepsy

Unaware

Epilepsy flows freely through me
This would never be easy for you to see
When this creeps silently towards me
And there is nowhere to flee
For I continue to beg and plea
To lend me the only key
To set my mind to be free
And start my life seizure free

Do Not Judge

What is there really different to see?
About anyone including me.
Many wonders what may be wrong
When these seizures occur so long
And learn to take them and juggle
Even during our times, we struggle
As we been hit with a knife
For our seizures became part of our life
And we are all unique in our own ways
When there is nothing more to say

A Part Of Me

Epilepsy has been a part of me
Yes, I had seizures since I was a baby
So, you take it or leave it
Because it may never go away
And may be here to stay
But doesn't make me different
From other children around
However, you may ask if I'm ok
I may reply and say yes
Even during the times, I jerk around
Dropping down may not be so good
When you may never realize
How much epilepsy became a part of me
Which makes me unique
In many different ways
Reminding ourselves to never give up
Because quitters may never win
And winners will never quit
For I have chosen to be a winner
To never forget who we are
And who we have become
As we get better and better

Trying To Escape

There are times it may be hard to escape
When feeling of being in outer space
I begin to ask what is wrong with me
As I become blinded and unable to see
Nowhere left to steer
For my fear becomes so near
No one would understand or know
As my side effects begin to show
My vision gets fuzzy seeing doubles
As if I saw many bubbles
I wish nothing but for this to go away
As I do not wish for this to ever stay
A cure is waiting to be found
For doctor's search all around
Hospitals can make you feel alone
As you seek a new milestone
And take a new life to reshape
As this condition is hard to escape
When feeling in outer space

The Unknown Awareness

Do you know what it feels like
When not knowing about your next seizure
That will creep upon you from no where
As this becomes one big struggle
For I have built fear within me
From doing the things I dreamed of
When I tried to life my life normal
Have the scars this would leave me
As this was a part of my life
And I continue to pray for answers
That there would be that one day
When doctors would tell me this great news
That I would become seizure free
And free from the medications
To living my life to the fullest
Without any worry of having a seizure

I Continue To Pray

I think you may never see
The times I want to flea
When I sit down and pray
For this to come to an end one day
Even when in need of a second hand
When you may never understand
The struggles this comes with
As you may things it's all a myth
With nothing left to be said
For you witness my eyes behind my head
When the seizure creeps on me
And you begin to see
What I really go through
As if you were in my shoes

Seizing Again

Here I am again going into this haze
Unsure if I would get out of this maze
Or when I would get out of this fit
As it leads me frightened, confused for a bit
Just know this, when I do
During this time, I may not recognize you
For this takes me more by a surprise
And the headache awaits to rise
We all have hope for doctors to say
That they will have a cure some day

The Overactive Brain Activity

Neurons overactive moving in all directions
For the cause of seizures with no detection
Seizures after seizures causing memory lost
The feel of life being taken and tossed
Waking up either in a hospital or on the floor
When barley able to walk out the door
Without the helping hands of someone
As things seemed to become undone
And learn to move over those bumps
When feeling down in the dumps
As the seizures begin releasing
And the symptoms begin increasing
For there is nothing for you to do
As this is something, we go through
When there is nothing to do but to wait
For things to get straight

I am Here

I am here seizures
You may have not won
For the damage you have done
You seize me day and night
When I have to continue my fight
My mind has been confused and tricked
As a seizure appears so quick
You strike and my breath becomes no more
When I will soon be able to open the door
You will have no victory still
When I no longer have that awful pill
And you can never seize my soul
For I have reached my goal
When I will no longer have that feeling
Creeping upon me from my believing
As I continue on my run
When I know you have not won

In The Shadows

Epilepsy is a disease in the shadows
Looking up into the afterglow
When reluctant to admit to our condition
For we begin to seek ambition
As our shadows let in light
When our lives begin to become so bright
As we continue to fight this mystery
For this becomes part of our history
And this mystery condition won't let me down
When I pray and will not be left to frown

I Don't Want

I don't want your pity
Neither want your sympathy
I wish for you to bend
Do nothing but be my friend
But to give me a lending hand
As this time has not been planned
And this moment has been really rough
When life becomes really tough
Please don't turn your back against me
As I may feel cold and lonely
So please don't give me your pity
Or give me your sympathy
As this has become part of my life
And there is very little I could do

Little Fighter

Hey there little fighter
Soon things will be brighter
Let your heart continue to sing
As we fight through this whole thing
And never stop believing
When times seem so deceiving
So please never give up
And continue to keep your head up
As this is not the end
When you now have a new friend

Lift Up Your Arms And Pray

Lift your arms up
Let your spirits light up
As this is not the end
When the fight only begun

Don't let this take you down
For you are strong in faith
That your prayers will be answered
From the one and only God

He will continue to look down
And hold your hands
When he begins to pray
Until the end of the fight

For we continue our search
For the end of this fight
When we can live free
And become seizure free

He Doesn't Understand

For he who doesn't understand
With the struggles we face
During each episode without a trace
When this comes all in two's
As people begin walking in our shoes
When this becomes our life foundation
Fighting for the end to our condition
As we can once be set free
For the life ahead we begin to see
When we try to live our lives best
As we put this all to a rest
For those who may never understand
The time we have to spend
To pray for all this just to end

Never Give Up

Lift your head up in the sky
When those tears make you cry
As we pray for that one day
When we can live life in order to stay
For the struggles we have to face
Unknown to the next without a trace
And to find peace of mind
For something we want to find
As our fight comes to an end
When we can once gain a friend
And begin to ride the tide
With each other on my side
When I can once live free to be
To the time I become seizure free

Like a Breeze

Life seems like a breeze
During the times we stop and freeze
As we are unable to move
And take our life and groove
For the days that are so long
We step back and be strong
As we begin to live our life free
For those who are unable to see
When unable to live our life like a bird
As they think your nothing but a nerd
For they do not know you
And understand what you can do
When this makes you frown
Knowing this won't take you down
As we watch the leaves in the sky
And continue our lives and begin to try
To lift up our heads
From the tears that are to spread
When we continue to pray
That this will end one day

My Life With Seizures

Yes, I had seizures
And yes, I am a fighter
As my life becomes brighter
When I begin to shine that light
To put an end to my fight
For this has put a toll on me
When unable to understand or see
As I hoped this was just a myth
For the struggles that it came with
During each and every day
When I can continue to say
That I live my life seizure free
With no one to understand or see
For the person I am today

Don't Let Them

Hey you! Yes, I'm talking to you
What are you going to do
Don't let others make you frown
And let them put you down
For they haven't walked in your shoes
With nothing better to do
As life becomes really frightened
And the end of the tunnel becomes brightened
For you are to continue strong
Even when days seem so long
For the time you are spending
To find a cure to the ending
Of your seizure condition

My Story

I live life today
To tell you my story
As I become seizure free
To blow other people's minds
For many may never understand
The struggles I have went through
In order to tell my story
With my seizure experience
And to bring upon awareness
About the unknown of this condition
When I never gave up
From my faith and prayers
For the day I can say
I am seizure free today

There Once A Little Girl

Once there was a little girl
Sitting on the cold hardware floor
Unaware of her senses and surroundings
During the times of an episode
For the few minutes it lasts
Feeling like it never ends
When the auras begin to kick in
And others looking at you weird
As they do not understand
What this little girl is going through
Before they come to realize
That this little girl was me
Who was having those seizures
And trying to live her life like
The rest of the kids around
To live up to life's fullest

Questions To Be Answered

Waiting in the quiet room
For answers I want to hear soon
When this end becomes so near
That I will no longer have to fear
And as my heart begins to race
As I take my life and begin to embrace
When everything seems to go down hill
And I stand there at a stand still
Letting this all take a toll
When letting it go within my soul
Causing an increase of a feeling
When giving me some type of healing

The Price of Epilepsy

Many things have been lost
As this came with a pricy cost
When my life was full of fear
And learning how to take it and steer
For my cure will once be found
When I no longer have to hear that sound
For the closing of those doors
As I continue sitting on the cold wet floors
When these seizures begin to unwind
And the feelings become so unkind
For I wish to run for the hills
As this will leave me in a stand still
With nothing left for me to gain
As I suffer through all this pain

The Wonders

I often sit and wonder
If there ever be a cure
To the end of this terrible disease
As I grew into my childhood years
Unsure of what my future holds
As my seizures and medications increase
And my life spirits would decrease
For I had no control over this
From my daily activities
Living from all other kids
When unable to do other activities
Knowing the risk of having another seizure
Coming anytime unannounced
Until the day this will be all missed
When I can learn and grow
Each day seizure free
Without the wonder to
When my next seizure will be

Why You Leave Me

Who are you? Leaving me here
Trapped here with nothing but fear
As these times leave me in great pain
With nothing left to gain
I sit here wanting to scream
Knowing you took me from my dream
To the time I began to fall
Unable to stand up straight and tall
When you don't believe this is true
For you have not walked in my shoes
I take this as part of my treasury
When I tell you, I had brain surgery
Please don't let your lungs fill with air
As this cure is very rare
When I spent my time and cried
Knowing I did nothing but tried
From the years and time, I had to spend
In order to put all this to an end
For now, you are able to see
How this has set my life free

In The Darkness

Deep into the darkness
Long I stand alone
Wondering and doubting
Dreaming and fearing
What the future holds
No mortal ever
Dared to dream of
As I fight this fight
To my very end
For I am unsure
From the future introduced
Clearing my darkness
That surrounds me daily

Fight With Me

At the root of all this
My mind begins to hiss
Whether this affects your heart
And you watch me fall apart
Even during my stillness
This is still my illness
When it gets out of hand
As you may never understand
For this has entered my soul
As I fight through this as a whole

I Am The Storm

Here I sit down
Starring at the unnerving sight
You cannot withstand the storm
When you become that frighten soldier
Left behind for that attack

I sit here fighting my frown
For I begin to brighten my light
As my life begins to transform
When this all comes to a closure
And the warrior begins to whisper back

For I am the storm

Printed in the United States
By Bookmasters